Moon without Craters or Shadows

Moon without Craters or Shadows

Catherine Cobb Morocco

Kelsay Books

ISBN 13: 978-0692240816

Cover art: Adrienne Robinson

Kelsay Books
Aldrich Press
www.kelsaybooks.com

Acknowledgments

Many people contributed encouragement and feedback as I wrote *Moon without Craters or Shadows*. Thank you to my editors, teachers, family and friends. To Kathleen Spivack, for her brilliant, discerning eye and ardent belief in this project. To Tom Daley for toughening my writing and to the members of Tom's advanced seminar for critiquing many revisions. To Afaa Michael Weaver and to Holly Zeeb, Adrienne Richard, Ilene Rudman, Ellen Siegel and Carol Siemering and poets of Monhegan Island, Maine, for their comments on the poems. To Jan Bailey and Ottone M. Riccio ("Ricky") for launching me.

Doctors at Massachusetts General Hospital helped me survive to tell the tale, including Drs. Clark Chen, Sameer Sheth, Catherine Lavigne and Andrew Cole. Doctors in my family—Hans Neville, Margaret Neville and Fredric Pieracci--consulted at critical times and Fred read the full manuscript. An unknown nurse cradled my hand so I could start writing in the Intensive Care Unit. Judith Birnbaum listened and asked to touch the holes in my skull. My family wove a cocoon of attention and caring at every stage and attended readings. Adrienne Robinson created collages, including the cover image, around several of the poems.

These journal editors first published the following poems, sometimes in a different version:
The Massachusetts Review: "Bite the Hand"
The Spoon River Poetry Review: "Son's Story" and "Daughter's Story"
Salamander: "I Steered Clear"
Naugatuck River Review: "Bone Beauty"
Atlanta Review: "Pulpit Ledge"
New Monhegan Press: "Island Morning"
Island Voices 2 (Forthcoming): "Ledges," "Balances," and "Ashes"

The Dana Foundation for Neuroscience in New York selected "Son's Story" as the first winner in its search for poems that "convey thoughts on the brain." The Vermillion Quartet performed the poem in a choral setting composed by artist and composer, Martha Bancroft.

Finally, I am forever grateful to my husband, David, for his constant vitality and love.

CONTENTS

Bone Beauty

Here, hollows rounded as your thumb
lie in the bone.
Across these little bowls, skin stretches
as on tambourines or drums.

Soft places on a newborn's head
will disappear as baby plates fill in,
but these entrances will never close
over the sponge and labyrinths below.

Don't wait until this bone lies underground
and only curious diggers can explore
my skull. They'll find the usual holes,
surprise, these openings too.

Come, while there's time for you to know me.
Let me slide your fingers. Press
these little pockets here here hear.
Tap tap new music on this broken crown.

WAKING IN THE HOSPITAL

We Were Smiling

Instead of facing into the camera,
we are turned toward each other.
Your arm stretches along my back,
touching my hair.
Your fingers crook my shoulder,
pulling me into you as your eyes

play on my mouth, parted mid-syllable.
Our faces glow from exploring
villages in the sun.
A door, painted Mediterranean green,
stands open to one side.
Stairs with blue geraniums rise on the other.

Do you hear the shutter click?
As you smile at my lips parted mid-syllable
and pull me toward you,
the bleeding behind my forehead
that will erase my words and my hair
has already begun.

The Hole I Made

A shadow over a crater:
billowing spun glass,
blazing radiance from a deeper place.

My body splays, the fingers
clutch hot air and hair flies back.

Delirious in a first deluge
of sunrise on a frozen earth?

Toppling backwards,
I am already gone.

My silhouette, a space
left after heat dissolved
my face and bones.

These edges line the hole
I made when rendered ash.

Coma (My Story)

I sink to the bottom
grasses quiver in my face
minnow clouds silver and turn
into kelp snapping my feet
my arms scull hard enough
to pry me up from ink to rouge
my fingers press ice overhead   ice
belly up I watch blue shapes blear
hear cold sounds wobble
my hair scatters under glass
light willing to crack.

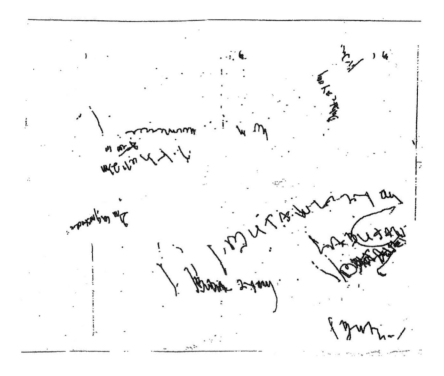

Intensive Care Unit. Scribbles

Intensive Care Unit. am i crazz what's wrronng

Intensive Care

the room spins out
smoke floats   walls spin
my hands   my feet   can't move
gagged my voice
I strain at straps

a man in white
"You want so much to speak.
Here, write to me."
He lays a paper on my chest
I cannot see it
unties one hand wraps it

on a pen up there
I cannot see my hand
pen scrambles   slides
how to guide my hand

slow   slow the pen
think think my hand to write
I barely move the pen
stay in a tiny space

    a m   i c r az z
"No, no the tubes are in your throat
to help you breathe Your hands
might pull it out."

My pen snarls
he winds me in the pen again
    w h a t w r o n g
"You needed brain surgery to live."
    h u s b u
Blizzard. Your husband's
walking here

when out
"When you can breathe alone."
I want to tell him I am somebody
  a writer   books
"You're interesting.
I can read you."

sits me up room whirls
man in white lifts out the tube
I can breathe
I hear my voice
We say goodbye goodbye
He says goodbye.

Sister's Story

For two nights
I press my fist
between the edge
of my fold-out cot
and your cranked bed.
Listening to drips,
monitor clicks.
Listening for you.
Cords coil into shadows.
Ambulances flash
red on metal tubes
draining your head.
When you open your eyes,
I take the train back
to oranges and flowers
on street corners.
You are breathing
in my belly.

Son's Story

I'm shaking scarves over my mother's bed,
where there's no evidence of thought.
In one of seven silken scarves, lithe women
sway around a mandala. Their skirts are painted
amber, apricot, and blue. Each sylph is named
after a continent: Antarctica's fur headdress flames,
blue dolphins leap, swim at her feet.

My mother's eyes are closed, while Oceana's
teasing head is crowned in grass and leaves.
She holds a plate of purple fish. I spread
Toros Magnifico around my mother's feet. A picador
thrusts his pic to pierce the bull into the ring.
In corners, matadors and bull horns' swelling.
Velvet ladies hurtle roses to the bloody kill.

Just lying here, my mother is a dreamless spot
without a nerve. I cannot stir her. Is she struggling
with shades? Will she open up her eyes to see the golds,
smell fish, flowers, blood? I tie a corner
of the bull fight to a corner of the dance, join seven
scarves into one rope, lands billowing. If I throw it,
she must cling. I'll pull her to her body, knot by knot.

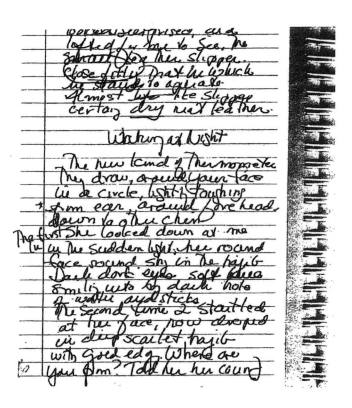

Dark dark eyes soft blue smiling
into my dark hole of water and sticks

Night Nurse

My room is pitch.
Her face clicks on, draped blue, forehead to chin.
Astonishing—a cameo with copper eyes.
Please talk to me.
She moves around my bed taking my vitals.
Flashlight off, buried again.

Another night, her hijab radiates ruby.
When I say my name,
she says her country is the same.
We chatter, faces almost touching
in the pool of light. The beam
illuminates the IV by my sleeping place

Tonight I watch her wrap my arm.
This time a purple scarf—just strings of beads—
rings elfin bells around her cheeks.
She circles with her chart and pen.
I cannot see her eyes.
She slips away, sinking the light.

brain dipped. They all wounded.

After Anesthetic

On my wall I see a broadside
advertising Betty Grable thighs.
They rise bare, dimpled, blazon
comedy for soldiers.
Starry chandeliers hang over satin seats
for swaggering men.
I hear her call out ribald jokes,
one then another, at the soldiers'
seen and unseen body pieces.
Laughter explodes with jokes about prostheses—
lean-wired jaws, steel feet. She lampoons
blokes mauled, left behind, 'til scarlet
rises up men's necks and faces.
Belly howling, wet-eyed soldiers
writhe with every joke she sounds.
I see men rise, buckle and groan, holding
their heads as though their brains are flying.
Lock their arms around each other.
Scatterings of men become one tight
fraternity of wounds.

What I Missed

on that night when I slipped
into slippery sleep. There was pot roast
and sisters all poised for a toast.

I missed auntie huff to the phone,
Davey calling my name. What a shame
I was sleeping and out of the game.

Someone rushed to the door. I was snoring
when men with long axes rushed in there.
Men swung me up high in a chair.

Then they carried me out. Someone
opened the doors of a square limousine.
What a scene! A fine scene!

But I missed the inside: dashboard, chromious
dials, fibrolators. And if we should float,
a smallish rubber boat.

We dashed through the neighborhoods strobing
our flashes. Jammed cars slowed us down.
We were bogged in the town.

Then the driver (who should get a medal),
gunned down on the pedal. Cleared trees
over cars at a speediest speed.

That's not all. In our fine limousine
we sailed down from the stars into lights.
Men ran toward us in whites.

Then I saw it. The sign blazing red.
Is this signal for me?
EMERGENCY.

MYSTERY

Bruise

Bruise by my left eye?
Good signs? bad signs?
Hand lotion where is it?
Heat?
Do I need air boots?
AIR BOOTS NEEDED?
Can I bend?
Why was the doctor wearing
galoshes?
Wrapped in handmade paper?
When the stitch is clipped
does it have a reverse memory
of when it was made?
Heat or ice?
What is normal?
Subdurals do become chronic?
Tylenol 5 hours okay?
What is normal?
Will I be able to leave?
Wash scalp?
Wine? Swimming? Sex?
Change my life? how?
A new bleed?
Three places?
Means?
A sieve?
Can someone help me?

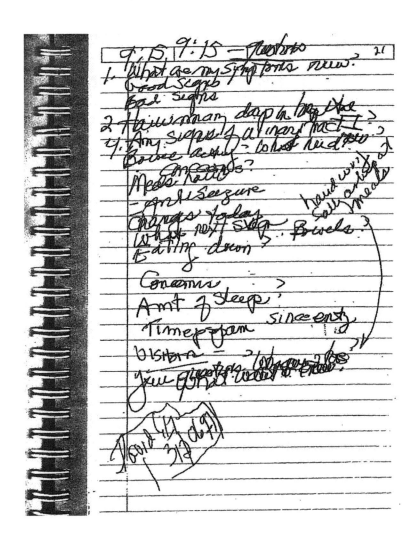

9:15 - questions
1. What are my symptoms now
Good signs Bad signs

Two Doctors

How should we care for her, what does she need?

    Her family thinks she's worried,
    all her deadlines are too tight.

The picture isn't clear. Let's wait and see.

    A dose of valium could be
    a key to quiet her anxiety.

I don't think that's the cause or what she needs.

    She asks her family, "What day is it today?"
    She never talks at meals or takes a bite.
    Aren't these all symptoms of her nerves?

They could mean something else entirely.

    What's more she thinks her mother's still alive.

All that confusion means her brain's not right.

    I don't agree. My theory's firm.
    She's stressed, emotions are too strong.

I'm sure it is a damaged brain, the scans
will surely show you my prediction's right.
You and I, we must agree tonight.

    We must agree tonight.
    Before it is too late.

We don't agree. It may be too late.

Silent Wave

They say that months before ferocious blizzards
freeze the cattle, muskrats thicken dens with mud
and cattails. Birds fly off and insects stop their chittering
before a savage undercurrent sucks up villages.
I hear that Miners' wives will scour their houses
long before the news of falling underground.
Like her. She lit off for the city five times in a month,
her back complaining bad, to see that child.
We told her, you've got years to know her, but the lady
had to see toys littering the rug like flowers,
bring arty books, cut pomegranates with the girl.
It must have been some mighty urge to make her board
that grimy train at night, just platforms flashing.
Could she know some silent wave would crack her?

Caves

My exhaustion starts in the vineyard,
winding with olive trees above Voltura.
I watch my husband and the others
bend to touch the throbbing grapes.
Juices sweeten in the sun until just
before they burst.

    I bought cases!
He assumes we'll drink it back home.
    Come see great vats, rose gardens!
    "I'm coming."
But I walk away through the rows.
Sit wasting against a warm stone wall.

The next day, we jolt through stark
wheat fields of Basilacata into Matera,
vast canyon carved by oceans.
    Come, explore with me?
    "I'll come."
I stand gripping the railing
high above a sea of caves.

The valley stretches in every direction,
pocked coral reef. He climbs
shattered paths around stone houses
built in crevices, stacking up slopes.
White except for shepherd smoke.

We stay in stone, glass rooms
carved out of caves where families
and their donkeys slept.
    After you rest, you'll rally, won't you?
He waits.
    Meet me?
I stall under a curved ceiling.

Riding Motorcycles

Doctors don't know
who will remember the kisses
what's causing the bleed
I'm trying to be impressive
if it sucks down the blood
smiling and laughing
something has changed
people have dreams like this
a bloom is ready to burst
my chest under the sea
my son carries his sadness

Doctors don't know
I saw my bare head
Kelly is really good with makeup
I can't print a straight line
what's causing the new bleed
how to get someone to mop
the expletives
where is my Burt's Bees overnight
crying brings us out of the trash
Doctors just say
don't ride a motorcycle

Brain Cells (Husband's Story)

How is she? I open bills I go to bed with Tylenol see what tomorrow
rains they're celebrating Christmas in the pubs anxious I'm alone
we drew her Christmas cards she couldn't see our six inch tree the
person that I know is gone in doctor world you barely function hey,
it's good enough but holy shit my wife's not here brain cells will
they kick off? a woman in the hall opens her eyes 10 seconds at a
time people could starve here drives me nuts I spoon feed her will
she aspirate? nuts then she wakes chats we take her home the
bleeding stops it starts again the nurse says here you are again they
look at blood kidneys inflection Ct scans they still can't find a cause
the doctors argue argue safe to operate again? brain cells will kick
is there a change? tell me should we operate? It's up to me??? she's
deep asleep somewhere if she's a vegetable my life will end we take
a chance I'm waiting at the pub a cell phone miracle she wakes up
singing how is she I never hope I open bills I go to bed be calm
see what tomorrow brings it's over or it's not we have a shot we're
fighting now holy shit she woke up yes she sang

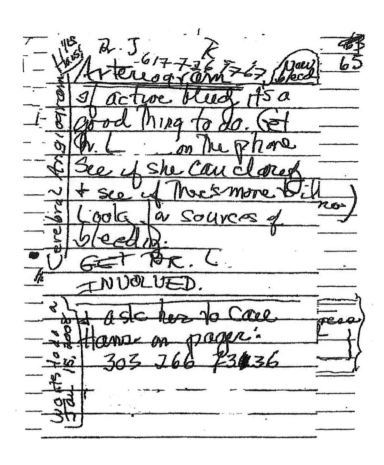

If active bleeding it's a good thing to do.

Alien

Lights sharp in my eyes. A chrome
colossal glistens in this basement

room. I've heard that ice is necessary
to maintain machines but I am

shivering on a stool, cold sheets
wrapping my neck and billowing

to the floor. Blue technicians
in blue masks are laying instruments

in rows beside the great machine.
Men will stare inside my brain.

A woman muffles through a goggle,
Other people don't complain of cold.

She clamps my head into a cage. In other
rooms some doctors watch my arteries

and veins alive and pumping on a screen
or tangled. Then nurse unlocks me.

Technicians fold up things. No doctor
comes to say if I will burst again or why.

Waiting for a Bed

They've shelved me on a gurney, freezing.
End to end a dozen line this chilly corridor.
I raise my head and see my feet pushing up tents
under the scratchy sheets. Beyond my feet,
a mass of auburn curls. She can't see me,
doesn't stir, Where are the windows, whirring
monitors to track our breath? Where are faces,
eyes? Just rubber squishing by. No mothers,
husbands, children scrape their chairs
up to our beds. No candy wrappers crinkle to the floor.
Where are the moans? Are seizures all on hold?
At least, if we were lifers we would tap the walls.
Dear curls, if I can warm my voice, I'll tell a silly story.
Once a shroud sat up, slipped off this slab.
He sailed to traffic, found a noisy bar and sang.
Please, call this story to the bald head at your feet.
Let's listen to the last head tatter out our tale.

Inside

As rounds of apple
cut crosswise through scarlet skin
show flesh and stars,
slices projected on the screen show
grey circles when old blood is dissipating,
silver streaks when new blood seeps.
Technicians snap these sections
when you rest your head on the machine.
I'd rather keep it all figures of speech:
"A brainy girl," "I've worked my brains off,"
to avoid the workings of the core.
Doctors exhibit one slice at a time.
My breath suspended, I wait at the screen.
It will expose the shades of light
and dark haunting me now.

IN THE NEUROLOGY UNIT

Daughter's Story

You're back. As though they plucked you
from a river, where you floated in the reeds
and over stones. Nets could not snag you.
Winds, currents pushed you further out.
People waded far to lift you. Purple skin,
your flesh was almost sponge enough
to separate from bones. Sticks in your
fists, a minnow thrashing in your hair.

I'm bathing you. Harsh lights go soft
on your transparent thighs. Your wooden
stool sits on hospital tiles under the shower.
You squeeze your eyes under your streaming
head. I wrap you in bleached, raspy towels.
Inside the room, more faces, flowers.
I tuck you dry and rising in the metal bed.

the Head - when without planning
it I saw my bare head on the
bathroom mirror my first
thought was

Moon without Craters or Shadows

Two eyes in a pale moon.
A hospital mirror, harsh lights.
Please God, let it not be me.
Hair, cheek bones, rose skin erased.

Something familiar in the outline
rouses a heartbeat. I must tell
my brother, it's the family head—
his, our father's. But only the males.

It didn't help that my husband said,
"You are magnificent!"
"Not many can wear bald."
Or that we joked that I'm the star

in a ward of head cases—
drooling mouths, lolling heads.
Or that our son made a collage
of power bald stars—Sinead and Demi.

Now, in the mirror, I see stubble
and faint contours of a nose and chin.
Shadow eyes, mouth crevice.
Sad face lighting the night sky.

Dear Medical Resident

If parrots fly out of my mouth
and vines push through the walls,
will you crack this frown?
If the nurses gyrate the Mashed Potato
will you lift your eyes from my chart?
Will you ever smile?
Look at your stitches crisscrossing
my skull like a drunken band.
Other docs, do they smile at your knots?
Go home, practice on bed sheets.
Go cleaver a broiler or two
through the breastbones,
stitch up all the muscles and skin.
Come, chat with children curled up
on my pillow with cell phones.
Lie back in a hospital gown barely tied,
then try sleeping with ghosts.

Bite

As I study petals clicking to the sill
and chimney pots angling outside,
it drags me by the neck.
The nurses give me pillows, Percocet .
"It's not related to your brain."
Have doctors looked at x-rays?
Teeth bore in my bone.
The nurse, "Imagine ripples,
don't forget the knees."
Shouldn't they look at x-rays?
"Use more ice."
Reality is blood pressures and
when they'll bite off the tail
left on my head.

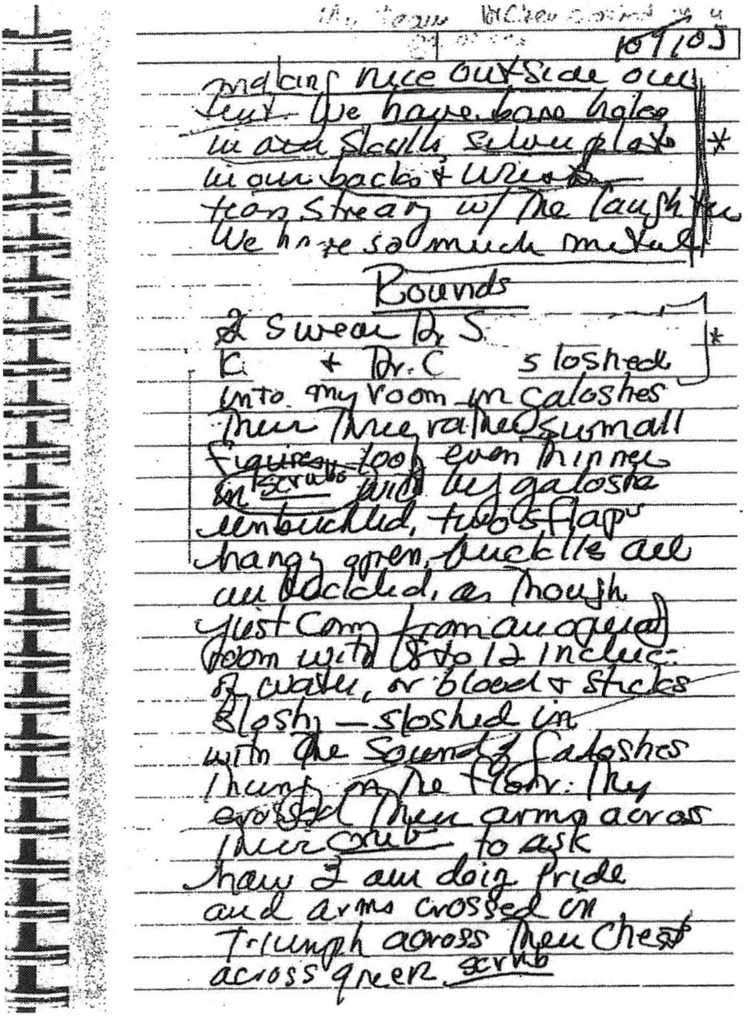

[handwritten journal text, partially legible]

making nice outside our
tent we have bam holes
in our skulls set up plates *
in our backs & wrists
tears streaming w/ the laughter
we have so much metal

Bounds

I swear Dr. S,
Dr. + Dr. C sloshed *
into my room in galoshes
their three rather small
figures too, even thinner
in scrubs with their galoshes
unbuckled, two's flap
hangs open, buckle all
all unlocked, as though
just coming from an operating
room with 8 to 12 inches
of water, or blood & sticks
sloshy — sloshed in
with the sound of galoshes
thump on the floor. They
crossed their arms across
their chest to ask
how I am doing Pride
and arms crossed in
triumph across their chest
across their arms

---

sloshed into my room in galoshes
buckles all unlocked, as though just coming
from an operating room with 8 to 12 inches of water
or blood and sticks
Pride and arms crosssed in triumph

My Team

They come bringing
their tools, each wearing
the same uniform.

The head man
brings a power drill,
tucked into his belt.
The apprentice,
a sharpened small knife.

The tall one carries a kit—
spools of black and white
thread, a scissor.
The last carries
work gloves for all.

Flushed with pride,
they circle the foot of my bed.
"Good morning!"

Neighbor

A curtain sweeps ceiling to floor between our beds.
Shoe soles move back and forth. Wheeled in
last night, each of us has a bed, one chair, a nurse.

While I'm in pain, my roommate's on the phone
bossing someone. Men come—husband, grown sons?
Their legs muscle the cloth as they crowd in.

I think they're somebody. She's ordering a table
for their take-in meal. Their talk is politics, the war.
They seem the kind who wave from cars.

She's on the phone, her voice balloons into my space.
I ask my nurse, shut off the lights. Order earplugs.
She must know I'm irate. Will she retaliate, call her sons?

"You're there?" she whispers from the dark but I won't
hear. At dawn, I shuffle past the grey gown and
the bare head sutured front to back like mine. "Hello."

Visitors

7 am
The flower Man
carried an amaryllis
blaring red into the room.
Give me gauze tulips.

11 am
I hold out my arms in front of me,
as if a sleep walker. The doctor nods.
Now close your eyes and hold your arms
out to your sides. He's working.
and he wants to know if I can keep
my arms even. I'm tilting in the wind.

11:00 am
They sit beside my bed in hard chairs:
a man and my grown girl, silent.
The baby turns away into her mother.
Sitting still, they dark their eyes
into me, like an old photograph.

2:00 pm
The new Transporter man, instead
of rolling me onto a narrow gurney
for our trip to more machines,
muscles my bed and all its gadgets
down the hallway. He shoves the bed
half-in, half-out of the metal doors,
setting off bells and flashes
as we shut down Elevators F and G.

5 pm
I never asked
the Hospital Psychologist
to pull up a chair.

See your friends
in crystal globes hanging
from strings around you.
All your people smiling.

In glass? Prowling
overhead? Dressed small
as fingers. Insects
captured in rare tombs.

10:30 pm
Light cracks the door
again my friend slides
into my bed after curfew,
past heads bent eating
from baskets at the desk.

Her sweater warms my chest,
slacks wrap my bare legs,
hair fleeces my cheek.
Listening to my wash of stories.
Listening, she slides
from our cave to a world.

Cool

After surgery my sister paints
my toe nails, finger tips St. Peters Burgundy.
A color usually reserved for velvet,
royalty, and wine.

My nails will startle rumpled gowns
we patients wear. A scattering of poppies
when the nurses lift my sheets
to take my blood pressure.

Tips, luscious red, peek out of slits
in air boots. Stopping more than one
technician taking me up the elevators
to an EEG, a Ct scan, MRIs and back.

I don't apologize that I stand out
in hallways lined with head patients less
daring, certainly, than I. One rakish hat
in church. I'm proud of all ten scarlet flags.

When my many doctors, young and buff
in scrubs, circle the bed tomorrow morning,
I will smile, knowing they see my lovely nails
and not the drains or my bare head.

Stitch

When the stitch is clipped and
pulled out does it have a reverse
memory, of when it first was
made, crunch or shoelace walked
on snow. Shifting slightly into the snow
grey snow... puffy
backs the skin which is all that we
ever wish to see, g the head.
Skin pulled... balance
between tight and taught —
such cream and rose
How is it, that until now
I never thought... what lies
beneath the structures & bone
+ sinews. No longer...
think outside. Love...
think, or have... the container
thought... the whole. the container
the soft, the hard, the elastic, the
... the tough push into teeth,
the soft into cheek..

When the stitch is pulled out does it have
a reverse memory of when it was first made, crunch.

Stitches

crisscross my scalp,
   as regular as tracks
of animals, embroideries,
   or skis when we tramp up
a mountain to weave back.
   Interrupt the flow of hair,
leaving raw thatch.
   Jolt visitors with thoughts
of matter underneath,
   in reach of doctors who can
cut through skin and skull
   if brain works down inside
go wrong. Latch doorways
   to calamities crouching below.

the peach pink-falling over the w [s] sills [My brain]
hand for writing is weird

The Other Side

My son brings butterflies—
    blue, coral, yellow, amber, white—

of silken feathers, captured from a
    photo shoot of hats for Vogue.

Tips filigreed with black vibrate.
    He drapes them over blossoms

on the sill. Outside bulldozers savage
    an aged hospital. Steel arms punch

walls, tear open remnants of dim rooms
    like my own. We watch masses of wings

lift off and melt through glass. Quiver
    and sink down to the wreck below.

Drift like confetti into ravaged windows,
    onto bricks severed and jutting into air.

Tapestries settle onto cranes ramming
    their jaws. Butterflies rise above the

tearing, shiver through the window
    to my bed, soft settle on his arms.

My son said, "I couldn't
understand. The medical
stuff. So I gave you
butterflies, scarves and
face cream for your
metaphysical self."

My daughter said, "After
three or four days you
were putting on makeup.
But then it happened
again — more surgery.
I realized I can never
take for granted that
you will be okay. Especially
the more vital side-spirited
energetic, adaptable parts.
Every time we came.
it was snowing. I felt
I was in a storm I
didn't know if you would
ever take care of me
again. I'm not ready
for that. I have to
depend more on my
friends.

My son said, "I couldn't understand
the medical stuff. So I have you butterflies,
scarves for your metaphysical self."

My People

Call dr. Lendle (sp?) Dr. Lin who do I call after hours but not the middle of the night? call Larry Lucas re: taking pain meds questions for Dr. Lin see Dr. Lin Fred says take it easy Nurse "Molly" Gee, I come back 3 weeks later you're still here! Dennie really good with make-up STAFF nurses are Molly, Dennie, Tara, Karen Dr. Lin - drugs Nurse Janet said "You will be getting back to full capacity" crackers? Dennie- in time we will know" Visiting Nurse will coordinate tell Dr. Lin-pain 2 new neurologists Nurse: going down hill a bit worried Dr. Sadaf says I'm still a mystery Penny Smith - VISITING NURSE Bonnie Angsyk (sp?) CASE MANAGER boss Daisy cleaning our house Watch Oprah Case manager AGUSSZYK My doctors are Dr. Carl Lin Dr. Sadaf Dr. Lindle Betsy PT Dr. Carl Lin called -- a new BLEED! Call Dr. John Radnor Radiology tomorrow arteriogram might reveal cause source GET DR. Lendle INVOLVED tell nurse I'm scared nurse: Leave jewelry at home Call Laura ask for solace Want to speak w/Dr. Lin about result Dr. Lendle Have you received results? Laura - You're doing well Wrote thank you to friends thanks Marcia veggies chicken Noreen thank Amarylis KIDS COMING!! Maria can clean Sue Worth speech therapist no ironing PREPARE FOR KIDS Laura says I'm doing well Dr. Carrie (Carolyn) Lendle says subdurals do become chronic

Dear Drs. Lin and Lendle: "As I continue to progress I am grateful to you and your MGH team for your persistent care and problem solving about each step in my treatment. Thank you for saving my life."

OUT ON THE HIGH WIRE

I Steered Clear

I steered clear of that basket of cards
for ten months. As if red hot, holding terrible news.
A hundred or more piled up, spilling.
Cards started coming. I was cold asleep
in a washed out room. A body, a bare head.
I was somebody before. Some called me the lead
female elk. Ears perked listening for men with guns.
Cards piled up when I lay back home looking
at branches from the window.
I moved back into things. Started opening cards.
Look at that. All hearts and rivers,
girls with curling eyes tossing roses.
Everyone I knew and didn't know saying
"valley of shadows," "terrible," "hope to see you up."
I get it. They were in there all along.
Trampling my room. Staring down at the wreck,
the rumpled gown. Circling the bed like wolves.
Some with pitiful tears. Blizzard of cards
saying, *We see you brought down.*

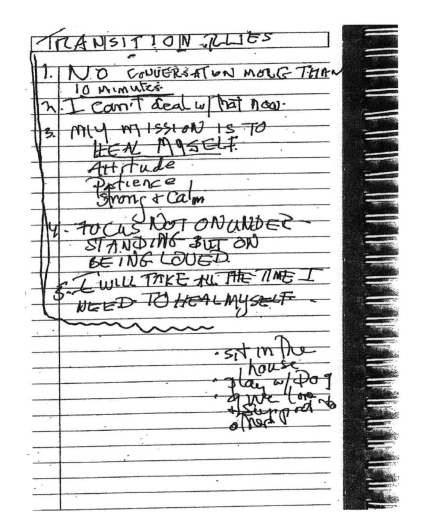

1. NO conversation more than 10 minutes.
2. I can't deal w/that now.

Asylum

I stay in my house
avoiding crowds, noises, falls.

North window—
Clapboards shred
neighbor's house
mailman lumbers up their steps.

South window—
Slice of garden
three graces naked with scarves
circle the birdbath.

Front door—
Maple shadows
dapple recycle bins
mailman steps up our walk.

West windows—
Verbena hides air conditioners
lushes fence
dulls vibrating tracks.

Home is sanctuary monastery asylum.
Risk-free guarded
tame.

The Cards

your condition gave us all the blues can't keep you down I won't call
life is upside down so many of us do without all these outrageous
dramatics exceedingly kicked the wind out of us holiday in the
mountains and valleys out here in Native American territory Trap
Day thinking (*what me was there*) mysterious course traumatic
and stressful navigate the Great Canal a mote in the thing of swims
return with fanfare camp out so many of us on the couch up and
running walking power no speed limit kick up amazing (*carried
me out in a chair*) up up up Moulin Rouge will travel resume enjoy
small gifts surrounded from Vietnam honor so many of us balm
(*I remember nothing*) more news a million emails thoughts constant
flow rooting what an adventure smile our shopping spree thank
you St. Jude peaceful days ahead (*thirty percent chance of recurrence*)
sing the unknowing don't clean the house visions of your garden
fashionable don't clean watch juicy foreign films a check for toes
and nails uppermost so many of us (*in separate houses writing to me
humming around me like water*)

Escape

Cheer cheer of cardinals
calls me from a grey place
where I hide my failures,
close my eyes from color,
spring from touch, cut off lights.

The trills grow harder to ignore.
They're dragging me from fracture
out to peonies and scarlet bodies
blazing against green.

The melody from one singer
echoes from another. Stunned
by counterpoint across trees,
I'm audience to chamber music
in a theater of sun. I mind my
soundless sleep again.

Ledges

You need a walking stick.
I lurch from one rock face to another,
study my footing, steadied by his arm.
Boulders, fallen pines threaten our way.
  At least until next summer.
We climb through purple flags, raspberries,
wild briar roses, past a deck slice caught
upright between boulders. Tugboat
bow and smoke stack scatter over ledges,
sheer above swells.
  You think I treat you like a child.
Sun flares through razor openings. Rust
runs blood over decay, lacework.
  But if you crack your head,
  I'll be the one to pick the pieces up.
Just today.

Glass

Someone else's water glass,
her crystal candlestick,
a chimney for a kerosene lamp,
splintered in my hands today.

Bits stick and hide and in rented rugs.
But it's my husband's coffee pot—
grounds bleeding from the crack
that seals the evidence.

I hurl the walking stick. Slivers
of beer glass glint in sand.
I teeter on boards laid over mud
and trip on stones.

Cliffs sheer below me to a boiling sea,
surf shatters into sparks.
I'll hide under this overhang of granite.
Eying me, a gull jerks sideways.

My husband will say, "It's not so terrible."
I'll say, If there's glass, I'll find it.
"We can do the hard parts.
Glass is plentiful. It's cheap."

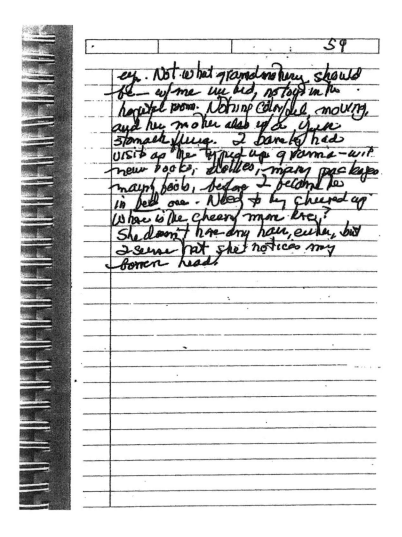

not wat grandmothery should be—w/me in bed
I barely had visits as the typed-up grama—with new books

Yaya

The other grandparents gave themselves
the old names: Nana, Nano. I waited for her
to name me, while her parents offered Gram
and Gigi. Finally she called me something
and I took it. Then I went underground.
Since I've come back, she'll hold my hand
at corners. Lets me catch her
at the slide when dirty boys leap on.
Was it my stubble? Stooping walkers
in the hallways? Funny smells, white coats,
her mother's twitching mouth?
How could she understand that I lay
tangling in the river and had to let her go?
Her father points to me, "Who's that?"
She looks at me now but never says, Ya Ya.

1ˢᵗ → Dr. D — Jho (Jo)

March 13 Dr. E — follow
up to March 12 CT scan

Driving
Legally six months
from seizure = aug 3rd
Swim — 4 months more
= end of July
Travel car + train — OK
Air travel = September 6 mos.
but get cleared by Dr. C
before

→ If we drive to Santa Fe,
get cleared before we
go — see April apt'ment

If end up at N.Y. Presby
See Will Curry's father —
neuro surgeon on staff

If have trouble in NYC
go to emergcy world

Have 6-8 interval to
next CT scan = April 25 &
24

Driving Legally six months If have trouble in NYC
go to emergcy ward

Driving Again

Have I ever seen this car before just get inside whose hands are these locked on the wheel this small bundle of lines across the gearshift which is backwards why three pedals for two feet telephone wires drape under sparrows blossoming red lights greening at the corners I won't rush but cars jerk honk around me eyes swim by fumble the down button I hear the open mouth You move it lady jerk I'll slide down in the seat and disappear peer through the steering wheel tanks grind around my car store windows slide by white shirts suck into film giraffes too big for mini skirts sidewalks roll backward under running legs I'm ready please to turn back home but unfamiliar gardens bricks float by boys bicycles in crosswalks sun explodes through branches shuts my eyes splinters railings tulips windows clear hot light flashes again dissolves swing sets boys smoking bicycles

which pedal is the stop foot

After Falling

I'll step toward the stairs
holding a heating pad
and a film flips on:
I'm catching a foot in the cord,
sailing, arms out on a trapeze.
Wallpaper rushes me roses.

I turn it off with a mantra:
Don't go there!
Say I'm pushing my granddaughter
to the park and an ordinary cab
turns the corner and I see it
Don't   the cab hurtling   Don't go!
toward us   There.
But just as I'm on my way again,
some circuit loops me back
to flying stairs, a flaming stroller.

Right now, I'm peeling avocados,
scraping bits of peel into the disposal,
digging my hand down   Don't!
and I watch someone   Don't go
flip the switch.

What Remains

I noticed pretty things—
a blue-green opal in the path
as I flipped on a tree root,

red alligator sandals rushing
toward me when I stooped
and toppled backwards.

I judged the distance to the ground
my landing place, body part,
my chances of survival.

I prayed that eagle wings would
scoop me as they rescued Gandolf
when the Dark Lord hurled him.

Or my own wings would lift me
as they did when I was ten
and sailed above the blinking silos.

Spendthrift dreamer. Yet
I have survived. Now what remains?
Terror that I easily dismissed.

Some life long aching muscles,
mending bones. Most of all, the silos,
red sandals, blue-green stones.

EVERYTHING IS DIFFERENT

Bite the Hand

He says I should express more gratitude
to those who dogged my brain waves,
carved my skull, parked by my bed for days.
What surly words, my churlish attitude.

Why should I lay out cakes to celebrate
my saviors? Bow my head to charity,
replay the lame one, scrape up pity.
No more drooling with the desperate,

or fawning at my caretakers. I fight
for comrades, all we nearly-cold survivors
raging at our crash. We stay alive
growing hot blood, new bone inside.

Won't waste my voice with humble bleating.
Won't erase the choler from my healing.

Before I Bleed (Collage)

I could never fight wild elephants at my doorstep
    like this woman, riding on a demon
battering her house. From layers of photo cuts
    she plants the long bone of one leg, presses
her toes into the leather back to balance.

I could never hold this animal from splintering
    my door. I couldn't rouse the cutout people
sleeping in the borders. I would send out
    messengers with flowers to plead, or I would
climb a tree until the fray subsides.

If I were pasted in here, could I dodge these whirling
    tusks before they razor me, before I bleed?
Before the body slams me I see myself leap
    from the frame ripping and pulling tusks, flanks
after me. I'd scissor them and paste them in a cage.

Just before it slams I see paint thicken my neck
    and thighs, fire up my eyes, the woman dragging me
up on the heaving back. We'll ride, hammering
    the head until the great legs buckle and the body
folds in piles of ivory and hide.

Ashes

Here, you tell me,
Scatter my ashes here.

Under our boots, lichen
smears the boulders crimson,
giant coals smoldering.
Seas glitter, radiate into air.

But where do think you'll be
as I unlock my hand,
release your ruins on headlands—
feathers drifting over cliffs
into the roil?

Will you dissolve, forever quiet
in ribbons of foam unraveling
beyond the surf?

Or will you prowl the hillside,
rustling red Wygelia by my cabin,
steal like mist
through cranked windows,
scatter my pens?

Speak to me.
Say you won't return
a mad mewing gull, unblinking,
one of the violent rude.
Spill like blood from icy crevices.
Survive this stone.

and know, that crying
brings us out of the trash
and sticks. how did this
crying to heal survive and
become a part of being
human. like the float,
pulled under the water by
the caught fish, suddenly freed
goes up and float free and
light on the surface of the
water. crying frees the
plastic float from the dark
deep swim shadow so that
it bobs playful again
bobbing by the water
what perfection of this body
that in addition to the pain,
the exhaustion, we found
tears and release. have
we always had this
weep rise through the
deep murk, air surfaci
hands claw up from
the sticks, mud, leaves.
dark water.

Crying brings us out of the trash and sticks,
frees the plastic float from the dark deep swim shadow
so that it bobs playful again

Balances

Unseen sculptors
formed these
fragile balances,
brown, gray
coral remnants
of this mountain
in the sea.

Cairns stand forever
along headland trails.
We move
around them
as Himalayan climbers do
on passing
prayer flags
tied by monks.
Om mani padme hum.

Held back
from entering this place
to build my father's
monument,
I watch a black cat
slide ahead
through buttercups, iris.
Satin shadow
swimming
among stones.

Three Harmonies

We don't ask,
what is that wing feather doing,
where are the feet?
as the whole hawk sweeps and curls.

Except at the beginning,
when the beak pierces the shell
and stubble gawks from a crack.

We don't say,
her heel is turning, her gaze shifted
as the woman circles, one body
moving in the ancient script.

Except at the beginning,
as I flat stand before my teacher,
my arms askew, thoughts dragging.

First lesson: He speaks as he moves:
Legs apart, arms down. Lift the right
wrist, turning. Then me? *Practice.*
What?

Second lesson: Turn, lifting the right wrist,
and the left wrist. Right arm inside left.
Elbows heavy. Then me. *Practice.*

His gesture evaporates before
I begin. The tail constantly
disappearing behind the comet.

Third: Turn, lifting wrists. In turning
shift weight back onto right leg.
Right arm inside left. *Practice.*

Across the room, ten-year students
move as one eagle, falcon, then forms.
New neurons, how soon?

Eighth: Turn, shift weight onto right leg.
Right wrist inside left. Palms open to center.
Elbows always heavy in Tai Chi
He draws with invisible ink

Fear Erases Things

I erased a barn today
as I walked past thinking,
the meadow is a long way down.

Erased the doors, edged white,
so dazzling the red faded
to vertical and horizontal stripes.

I duck into a thicket leading to the meadow.
Twigs crackle at my head, my arms.
Will I be bramble-trapped in here?

Sun filters through branches slicing
shadows. Now it flickers out
and iridescent ferns roll into dark.

I wake to thorns burning my hand.
Walk into the meadow just in time
to see a hawk tilt in an updraft,

just in time to see cross-currents flatten stems
with brushes into golden patches,
warblers or voles rustling beneath.

Blue grasses ripple, surge
around my waist then tighten like a belt.
I cannot step, I'm losing breath.

My mind erases grass before it loosens.
I erase the sun.
I don't know if that hawk dived for juice
or if the warblers clattered.

Rescue

We stretch a the rock ledge to see
the indecipherable glyph—deep strikes
and cross marks—in granite rising
out of the sea. We rowed to this island
this morning. Climbed rocks and crouched
in surges of heat and wind as a helicopter
lowered a basket to practice rescues.
A ship, loose as flotsam, months off course,
once cracked here. Viking, Phoenician or
a Celtic swan boat came with hide sails shredded,
iron nails ground into cross timbers.
Men tangled, terrified of sailing to the edge,
planted their feet, felt their bodies' heft.
Did they scratch graffiti in drunken jubilation?
Signal comrades foundering in seas,
cry out to a universe of water and gloom?
We trace their lost message with our fingertips.

.

Falling from Trees

We found this nest, smaller than my fist,
perched on blades of wet grass. Teal feathers—
a strange bird? scavenged angora?— wrap the outside.
Milkweed-soft rabbit fur curls in the bowl.
Bronze grass, fine as a woman's hair, binds feathers,
braids the rim. Broken threads fan into air.

How did this lacework, high, invisible,
holding an impossibly small egg,
survive the deluge and the cracking limbs?
And in my head, can sponge and jelly, crisscrossed
with veins and arteries, live in its torrent?

About the Author

Catherine Cobb Morocco's poems are published or forthcoming in *The Massachusetts Review, Prairie Schooner, Spoon River Poetry Review, Poet Lore, CALYX Journal, Sow's Ear Poetry Review, Salamander,* and others. Collections: *Island Voices 2, Unlocking the Poem* (Riccio and Siegel) and *Do Not Give Me Things Unbroken* (Ayers et al). "Son's Story" in this volume won the first prize for poetry about the brain from the Dana Foundation. An early music group performed the poem in a coral setting. Currently, Catherine is working on a collection of poems about her South Dakota childhood.

Catherine is the author of two books for educators, *Visionary Middle Schools* (Teachers College Press) and *Supported Adolescent Literacy* (Jossey-Bass). She has worked nationally with teachers on using writing to develop adolescents' deep understanding of literature. She taught at Clark University and has a doctorate from the Harvard Graduate School of Education. Catherine lives in Newton, Massachusetts.

About the Cover Artist

Adrienne Robinson works in a wide variety of media – stone sculpture, fabric and paper collage, acrylic painting, and mixed media. After having successful brain surgery, she found that creative ideas and work were pouring out of her.

She describes the collaboration with Catherine: "I worked completely from the subconscious, not planning and organizing, just picking papers and letting forms come forth. Working with Cathy with her vivid images was a perfect, fulfilling match." Adrienne lives in Newton, Massachusetts.